WACKEN

FOR BEGINNERS
2019

WACKEN
FOR BEGINNERS
2019

Regine Rauin

Copyright © 2019 Regine Rauin
All rights reserved.
ISBN: 978-3-948041-06-9

Translated with **www.deepL.com** -Translater

DEDICATION

I dedicate this book to all those who courageously set off on their way to HOLY GROUND WACKEN in order to pay homage to the spirit of WACKEN for a few eventful days without restraint, peacefully and joyfully ecstatically.

CONTENTS

Contents

DEDICATION 1
CONTENTS 2
ACKNOWLEDGEMENTS 5
PREAMBLE 7
1 - WHY THIS BOOK? 11
2 - WACKEN? - WHERE AND WHAT IS IT ANYWAY? ... 15
3 – WHAT'S THE IDEA BEHIND WACKEN? 21
4 - PREPARATIONS 26
5 - MANY WAYS LEAD TO WACKEN 34
6 - FINALLY ON HOLY GROUND 39
7 - CARE - PACKAGE 47
8 - CLOSING FACILITIES WITH CIRCUIT AND OTHER THINGS TO MENTION 53

9 – FOLLOW THE VIBES	57
10 - INCOMING CONTROLS	59
11 - OUTFIT	61
12 - LIFE ON THE MEADOW	63
13 - TOILETS & SHOWERS	69
14 – FOOD & DRINKS	72
15 – THE VILLAGE	74
16 - THE SWIMMING POOL	83
17 - SHOPPING	85
18 – WHAT'S YOUR FAVORITE BAND?	86
19 - STAGES	90
20 – BANDS	94
21 - WACKEN WITH A HANDICAP	104
22 – SUPPORTER AREA	110
23 – EVENTS & WARMUPS	114
24 - SPORTS	118
25 – TIME TO SAY GOODBYE	119
26 – GET YOUR TICKETS	120
ABOUT THE AUTHOR	121
NOTES:	122

ACKNOWLEDGEMENTS

To all of you who have helped me at my
"FIRST WACKEN"
have been supportive in word and deed!
Many thanks to Daniela Ben Said, who made it possible for me
to visit WACKEN 2018 by giving me her tickets.

PREAMBLE

In my book projects, whenever I arrived shortly before the finale of my respective book, there has always been a moment when I realized that there is an essence that I have not yet communicated. Why should it be any different with this book?

This time the deep inner core of my message plopped up on Instagram in one of my posts mentioning my feelings about WACKEN. I'll just give you an insight of my Instagram posts here:

WACKEN 2018:

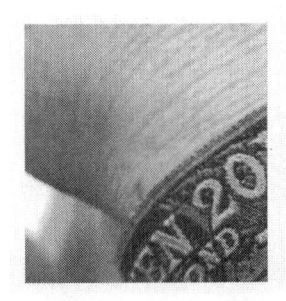

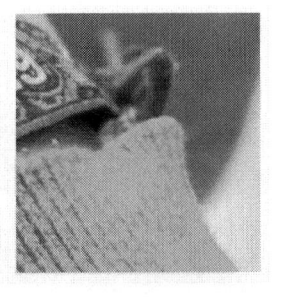

#Large picture #time! Why? Well, my #enthusiasm for my current book project #Wacken2019forbeginners and the underlying enthusiasm for #Wacken2019 is just too big to fit into a single picture. Due to the crazy #idea to start on day 38 before #WACKEN with a book that will #help you to enjoy your WACKEN this year...I got so deeply involved with WACKEN, its history, the idea behind it and finally the #soul of the #Festival, that I now understand so many other things and above all, why #hardrock has always been my great #love and why it - in my opinion - is experiencing a renaissance (rebirth)...because not only #colors and furnishing reflect the state of a society, but also its #music.

I think we've had a half-hearted, euphemistic, #ok tendency for many years: I've always said: "the music doesn't really climax". You don't have to worry about that with #heavymetal music. That's why the men are so masculine and the women so sexy...that's the point...and for those who get scared and rebel now, I recommend @veitlindau s #Podcast on the subject of "living your own shadow"...and because that's exactly what happens in WACKEN, WACKEN is so incredibly liberating.

It just occurred to me that #WACKEN is #wellness for the #soul, so to speak. All the grime and smudginess that's accumulated can go away. Anything not said, oppressed, can be yelled out, it's ok to feel yourself again, to rebel against conventions and to roll in the mud.

Like a clearing thunderstorm, like a real, honest argument that can be followed by an equally deep reconciliation that takes the relationship to another level...real is probably what it describes best for me...and because it's so real and there's no need for it anymore, to hide the "dark sides" of one's own self, there is a lot of room to accept and appreciate the others with all their corners and edges, good and bad qualities, because everyone is aware that he himself is not a "saint" and probably never will be. Well and that's the point where it becomes understandable why these over 75.000!! People who at first sight look quite frightening, can celebrate so relaxed and above all peacefully together. So let's go to #WACKEN2019 and free your SOUL!!!

...and the most awesome thing: #WACKEN is actually such a #protected room I'm talking about in one of my #Podcasts...that's just becoming clear to me...because what makes a protected #room is that there are clear #rules!

Much too often we have to lock ourselves in to feel safe, to find #quietness. This is important and perhaps the basic requirement for us to then move into such #rooms as #WackenOpenAir offers them.

WACKEN has the clear #advantage that you are not alone. Because even though I was there almost alone last year, I didn't feel alone at all. The clearly set rules (which are insisted upon...which unfortunately is not always the case when it comes to laws) give a lot of #freedom. If I - especially as a woman - can be sure that I am respected (because I respect myself) then I can really live the #Goddesswithinme.

Another, very important, somehow unwritten rule is that what goes on there stays there.

One of my biggest casualties is my former favorite pub. That doesn't mean it doesn't exist anymore...it just disregards some of the most important rules of the game by now: through the monitors that let everyone on the street participate in what's going on inside, inside NOTHING happens anymore...in earlier times only the waiters and we knew what has been taking place there (ok, if anyone could remember it at all) and exactly because it stayed among us, there was this unique energy that made the air vibrate...and the other thing: a lot of it's not real anymore...it's just that #energy that made the air vibrate...and the other thing: a lot of it's not real anymore...it's just a #fake in many cases... Too often I have seen completely bored visitors who suddenly staged "yeahh, we are having so much fun" for a #Selfie...hey, the real fun only evolves when your head if full of so many things, but definitely not to take a picture!!!

In this sense: have fun with this book and even more fun this year in WACKEN!

- Would I drive alone if I couldn't find anyone?
- What kind of luggage cannot be avoided? (I love to surround myself with as little ballast as possible, especially when travelling)
- Is it safe for me to travel alone as well?

Well, as feared, nobody wanted to come along ... and I should mention that one reason was that in my "normal" life I'm not necessarily surrounded by hordes of enthusiastic WACKEN fans ...

"Do I dare to drive alone?"

If such questions arise, I go through my personal worst-case scenario:

- I can't even find my way... (total nonsense, somebody will help me)
- Nobody is talking to me and I will wander alone through the area for 3 days (well, everyone who knows me personally will start laughing unrestrainedly at exactly this point...because I always find someone who talks to me - ok, with whom I talk... so, to whom I tell something...umhmm, I'll leave that like that...)
- Where am I supposed to spend the night? (That really had a point, because I didn't own a tent, nor did I feel like staying overnight. Motorhome was also non-existent, free accommodations would be at this time probably rather a laughing stock and in the evening, thus in the middle of the night, 40 km somewhere to drive, was not at all in question)
- It was helpful to answer the question: "How will the weather be?" Because the weather was without any doubt even there in the north with: "endless sunshine, temperatures around 30°C" announced...

Conclusion:

- I take a sleeping bag with me that can be crumpled together and sleep on the meadow, because if there is anything around WACKEN, then meadow (I thought at that time)
- I wonder if it's safe for me. Well, anyone who has ever travelled through some of Central America's hot countries - even with a partner - knows that "safe" is a very relative term. I remembered my eventful evenings in Düsseldorf's relevant hard rock pubs and then it quickly became clear: I have rarely felt so safe as in exactly this one! Yes, it may not look that way to the naïve visitor, but if some guy behaves badly in such a pub, he's out there faster than he can see...for women absolutely ingenious and unfortunately by no means everywhere the case...
- Well, it was still open: how exactly do I get there and where is it at all?...yes, I'm embarrassed too, but it will certainly happen to some others who ask themselves "where the fuck is this WACKEN at all" Because there's one thing you shouldn't forget: for the rest of the year WACKEN is a cute little totally tidy village, in the middle of nowhere (from the point of view of someone who lives in the centre of North Rhine-Westphalia...)

Well, also for this question there was an answer: People, in this case my classmate, ask what I should enter in the destination of the DB: Itzehoe was the answer. And in fact, very close, if you roll very close, you will find a place called:

WACKEN

After clarification of all these questions (clothes were quite irrelevant, because with announced duration 30°C it needs little to be happy...

I started to get a little hectic...

2 - WACKEN? - WHERE AND WHAT IS IT ANYWAY?

Let's just ask Wikipedia... that usually helps...But stop: the festival has also left its mark here:

Quote from Wikipedia:
Wacken is a community in the district of Steinburg in Schleswig-Holstein. The village is known for its annual Wacken Open Air music festival, which takes place at the beginning of August and attracts more than 70,000 visitors.

Not really satisfying... so here's a few facts:
  - Area: 7,1 km²
  - Population: 1,840 (31 December 2008) Author's note: and now? No one has counted for more than 10 years? Couldn't be...

Followed up just by stories about the festival – not the village...
so I took a look at the videos which are available on the internet to get a bit more knowledge about the village itself. That's the information I could get hold of:

Wacken - a village in heavy metal fever

DW German (04.08.2008)

Information obtained:

- Camping, if neccessary also in mud and mud (this is part of every decent rock festival)
Author's note: like this

- Wacken, a village in northern Germany and one of the hardest rock scenes you can imagine.
Author's note: spoken with the reporter's pronounced soft, sweet voice a la "are already pretty crazy who come here, but somehow also funny"

- reporter is - according to her own confession not a hard rock fan
Author's note: I would NEVER have guessed

- Stories (rim of the construction wagon broken off, a farmer had the right one and helped out)
Author's note: the heavymetaller is standing casually with the WACKEN T-Shirt of the Year at the entrance to this construction wagon with a can of beer in his hand

- Every year Thomas Hess is responsible for the stage construction. Important for the VIP's above the stage area: the expensive equipment must be protected from dripping beer...

- For the people of WACKEN, the Open Air is a kind of "Fifth Season".
Author's note: not only for the

- Voices of the residents: finally something happening here!
- Visitors are showered with garden hose by the inhabitants when temperatures are high in WACKEN.
Author's note: absolutely true and incredibly recommendable...just as much fun as shown in the report...

- The shops in the village do their business of their lives in these summer days...
Author's note: I believe so

- The employees have a strict vacation stop but a heart for Metalheads!!! Quote: "Super-friendly, nice, can wait!
Author's note: right and: wouldn't it be great if every customer would be a metalhead?

- What do they buy? Can ravioli, beer, water (for brushing your teeth)

- children of WACKEN learn for life: Transporting beer crates and are on their way to becoming a major forwarding agent...

- Thomas Jensen, born in WACKEN himself, has been with the festival since it was founded in 1990. His dearest child: the pit tower, to which you can go by elevator...
Author's note: I want to ascend it too

- Mystery: the festival has only been cost effective for a few years now (status: 2008)
and: WACKEN is only possible to take place in WACKEN

- Festival opening with the WACKEN Fire Brigade Chapel

- Farmer Uwe Trede rents out his fields as festival grounds and

earns according to rumors far more than with his dairy cows.
Author's note: tjooo, that 's already possible

- although his dairy cows are real HeavyMetal fans and give much more milk during the festival...

- farmer Uwe Trede also rents out the Dixieklos - the artists have buses with a better solution for the special needs
Author's note: but please don't misunderstand that

Conclusion of the visitors:

Look around, Metal brings people together, because there is so much heart and soul in it...this is something quite original
Author's note: exactly like this here.

Conclusion of the reporter:

...I've rarely experienced a more relaxed festival
Author's note: me neither

WACKEN - a visit to the village

shz.de - News from Schleswig-Holstein (04.08.2012)

Information obtained:

- Sievers bakery
- there are homemade muffins at Roswithas original WACKEN Muffins
- WACKEN helps (1 euro for the DKMS - German bone marrow donation)
- fish roll

WACKEN 2017 - a visit to the villagers

Kieler News (04.08.2017)

Information obtained:

- There are enthusiastic newcomers who didn't know what they were doing at first...and are now fully involved.
Author's note: I am deeply impressed: They are even able to form their hands to the common used sign for every metalhead: the fork!

- Very few of WACKEN's residents are against the festival. The few that are against are leaving for holiday during festival time or clean their plugs.

- The others suddenly miss all the visitors and feel suddenly alone after the festival, which they find very sad.
Author's note: I could imagine that some fans could be persuaded to stay for a while....

- Most of them have seized the opportunity of earning money with the festival themselves.
Author's note: true and that's certainly one of the reasons why most people are so enthusiastic about participating and are a real enrichment for all festival visitors....

- There are many great dear people there
Author's note: yes, me!!! – and a few others...

What about the Bild newspaper?

WACKEN 2018 - WACKEN in the mud

Information obtained:

- WACKEN is slowly becoming an adventure park for the pleasure-seeking metalhead.
- There's a cuddly disco where couples can have a quiet chat.
- Sports activities are also offered, e.g. charging mobile phones with muscle power.
- There is a stand with physiotherapists (Moshpital - Massage), who make tired metalheads cheerful again
- A seemingly endless selection of international food and drinks is offered.
- Attractions:

 Staying seated on a high stake: If you can hold out for six hours, you will receive an upgrade and can then enter the VIP area.
Author's note: I had the honor to be allowed in there in the evening - save the stake, the life on the INNER GROUND with all the metalheads is way more fun....

3 – WHAT'S THE IDEA BEHIND WACKEN?

Well, until they had the original idea in **1989**, Thomas Jensen and Holger Hübner, both living in WACKEN at the time, first had a drink and celebrated their friendship.

How could it be otherwise: the idea came to the two of them during this visit to the restaurant (ok, one of the numerous...comments of the author) very probably in an advanced humid-happy state.

Jensen played in the rock and cover band Skyline E-Bass. Skyline was one of the first regional metal and rock cover bands at that time. They had made it from appearances in village pubs as well as gigs at motorbike meetings to the support act at Extrabreit.

Hübner, on the other hand, played the parties as a disc jockey with a focus on rock music and heavy metal. So it was quite logical that the two of them had the great idea to organize an open-air concert in a gravel pit in WACKEN. Since the pit was also used by the motorcycle club "No Mercy's" as a venue for big meetings, it made sense to get together. Probably because of the totally central location

Author's note: little irony of the author...

it was decided that there would be an opportunity for visitors to camp.

In **1990** the two-day festival actually took place, but only with 800 visitors. At that time the necessary technology was set up privately on a trailer of a local forwarding agency. Beside the band Skyline played 5th Avenue, Motoslug, Sacret Season, Axe 'n Sex and Wizzard.

In **1991**, 1,300 visitors came and Mark Ramsauer designed the skull logo based on the basic shape of Thomas Jensen and Holger Hübner. What was the idea behind? Well, they wanted to show that they are "boys from the village" and that's why the cow skull refers to the venue: the cow meadow.

In **1992** it became really exciting, because the first internationally renowned bands performed in WACKEN: Blind Guardian and Saxon. The total number of bands rose to 26, including bands from Sweden, the USA, Ireland and Belgium.

For the first time there was a professional stage with lighting and the first sponsor: the cigarette brand Prince Denmark.

There was also a party tent for cover bands.

Due to the higher number of visitors, the festival moved to the neighboring areas of farmer Uwe Trede. He was to become another central figure of the festival in the next few years and has been a cult figure of WACKEN OPEN AIR since the film "Full Metal Village" at the latest.

In spite of all the highlights, the festival became a financial challenge, because after paying for garbage disposal and with the additional costs for the security personnel, the organizers were left with a loss of 25,000 DM - despite a number of 2,500 paying guests.

In **1993** Doro Pesch appeared for the first time and WACKEN OPEN AIR reached a new record of 3,500 paying guests.

Due to high losses, including the start as a local concert promoter, a serious accident involving Holger Hübner and the death of Thomas Jensen's mother, the year nevertheless went down in WACKEN's history as an "epidemic year".

In **1994** - the five-year anniversary - the financial situation stabilized: 4,500 tickets were sold and because of the everincreasing volume of rubbish with corresponding costs, entrance fees had to be paid even when entering the tents. Ticket reservations were rewarded with a free T-shirt as a small incentive.

In **1995** the financial situation remained stable, but profits were not made (except emotionally...author's note). The number of visitors rose slightly to 5,000 paying guests. Finally, the festival caught the attention of the media: Rock Hard magazine and the newly founded TV station Viva in particular reported on WACKEN ever since.

In **1996** things went uphill, but at the same time new challenges arose due to the everincreasing number of visitors, also in financial terms.

The first voices were heard in WACKEN, which were not so enthusiastic about being flooded by so many people every year. Uwe Trede therefore offered to take the entire festival, including the venue, to his premises and acquired further space.

Thomas Hess, who had been tour leader of the Böhsen Onkelz until then, completed the organization team, Sheree Hesse took care of the artists and VIPs.

1997 the W.E.T. Stage was added. Conceived for newcomers and bands who didn't have a record contract yet. The number of visitors reached the magic 10.000 and the band Rockbitch caused a stir with their erotic stage show.

In **2007** and **2008** the festival was already sold out due to advance ticket sales. The new goal was to reduce the influx of ticketless visitors, as the number of visitors in **2006** had reached 62,500 and thus exceeded everything that had been before.

In **2009** the tickets were already sold out by the end of **2008**, and the Medieval Stage was completed, where mainly medieval and folk bands played.
You better have a look at the names of all the bands on the WACKEN page at www.wacken.com, that would really go beyond the scope of this book, respectively it is not the focus of this book.

And what's it like today? - so what can you expect?
Today about 1/3 of the visitors and bands come from abroad and some of them arrive well before the festival starts.
Criticism of the hygienic conditions, the prices, the folders, the overcrowding and the commercial orientation of the festival was of course inevitable. The organizers improved in some places and for example contributed one million EUR to the extension of the local swimming pool and improved the mobile infrastructure.

Thomas Hess, the festival's production and former security director for many years, passed away on 5 April 2018. He made a major contribution to the festival's success and its good organization, peace and tranquility.

My first WACKEN (2018) was awarded **Best Major Festival at the European Festival Awards 2018** and **Helga! Awards as Best Festival.**
Author's note: I guess I made a great decision

In front of your first WACKEN 2019 (yeahhh!!) all 75,000 tickets were sold within the first four days after the start of sales. WACKEN OPEN AIR is now completely sold out for the 14th consecutive time!

Well, how does it feel to have purchased one of the much sought-after tickets - I hope, incl. T-shirt!!! - because this year will surely be history again:

30 years of Wacken!!!

4 - PREPARATIONS

What is going on with me right now? Well, I have set myself a big task: to write this book shortly before WACKEN OPEN AIR starts this year...to be exact: I started writing when the countdown on the official WACKEN OPEN AIR homepage was "34 days to WACKEN"...

You're daring, I know!

But it also has many advantages. One of them is that I don't have to come to you with such great slats, but can now supplement my unique fantastic experiences at WACKEN 2018 with the latest information of the original WACKEN – WEBSITE

https://www.wacken.com/.

To make sure this isn't such a boring lecture, I push myself every day before I start writing the next chapter by watching at least one video from the official site or on Youtube. Yesterday it was the official reports of the last years which are shown first... today I watched the trailer for this year... and it's just Genius!

Soo awesome that I would have liked to start immediately and would have helped there with the construction...

Well, maybe I can do that next year... that would be super genius... and maybe YOU will even be part of it... and I just lack any expression for that...here.

So, let's come to the preparations. Mine were short and concise last year:
- Make decision if I accept the gift of cards
- See where WACKEN is at all
- Book train connection
- Small backpack and packing my sleeping bag - and go...

Well, depending on the weather, this kind of preparation will also suit you, for safety there are a few more additions here...because after all, I'm a little smarter now and this book is there to lift you above the greenhorn status the first time, without anticipating everything... because you'll mess it up... that would be like a journey where you've already read all the details before, with the perfect pictures in front of your eyes and one insane (in the truest sense of the word!).!!) high expectation...That would definitely spoil your festival!

Hence one of the most important MENTAL preparations: WACKEN is perfectly imperfect!

What do I mean by that? Well, the WACKEN team is doing a great job, has the whole organization under control, which requires such a mega festival. The real hype is, however, that precisely because the setting is so well organized, there is plenty of space for the visitors - and they want to use it!

That's why I can only recommend to you: just let yourself drift, don't organize every gig, be courageous and just let go of your troupe (if you have one) and just let yourself drift over this area. Talk to people you've never seen before and enjoy the fact that the whole world is now guests at WACKEN. Sit down with others spontaneously in dust, dirt or mud, take a - as cool as possible - drink in your hand and enjoy being there.

Because that's exactly what turned WACKEN into such a great experience for me last year! I have spoken with locals, with outsiders, with boys and with "old people" with newcomers and with people who have been coming there for over 15 years. Just out of the situation... and sometimes I just sat there and watched!

Preparations!

It's great to have your own accommodation with you, but not a must. In the village there is a shop that offers everything your heart desires: tents, buckets, air mattresses, inflatable swimming pools and and and ...

If you want to enjoy the original WACKEN feeling, throw yourself on the campsite! The price is included in the ticket price - also for campers, caravans and all the other wild companions (let yourself be surprised, there is really creativity) Normally you can camp right next to your vehicle, unless the ground conditions do not allow it...

Since last year's running gag was: "I don't know what was worse: the mud 2017 or the heat 2018???" I decided this year to sleep on my trailer, because then I'm not lying on the ground, which can actually quickly turn into a single muddy landscape. After all, we are camping on agricultural land.

The campsites are marked with big letters - otherwise you wouldn't have a chance to find your home again... But even so, a WACKEN professional informed me right at the start that it's not unusual to miss your tent after all the experiences of the day and the corresponding fluid intake... and maybe never find it again.

My tip: in an emergency, just stay overnight under another awning, hardly anyone will resent you...or just stay awake....

The campsite is equipped with showers and toilets. These are also completely free of charge, i.e. included in the ticket price. They are also quite cool. If you can't sleep anyway or would like to refresh yourself at night, make sure you get there a little out of hours, the queues deserved the name "snake" last year.

Also included are signposts, light poles, breakfast tents, small supermarket tents, and some food and drink stalls.

For your preparations:

- Tent
- sleeping bag
- toothbrush
- towel
- washing things
- change of clothes according to weather forecast
- Sturdy shoes help
- You can even get rubber boots with the WACKEN logo from Metaltix on the Internet.
- By the way, there are special sales for Easter and Christmas in this shop (but this is rather the follow-up, or the preparation for WACKEN 2020)

During the festival days you can buy some merchandise in the **STORE** at Hauptstraße 82, 25596 WACKEN **+49 04827 999 669 99** (I am sure that you'll come by to explore the place anyway).

During the festival week the store is open around the clock from Monday to Saturday, on Sunday until 20:00.

It also functions as a **W:O:A Info Office** - the hub of the village outside the festival grounds.
There is even an ATM, merchandise until the end of the day, drinks and snacks and the possibility to charge mobile phones!!
It can be recognized by the W:O:A Tower (formerly Raiba-tower) in the background, so you're sure to find it! Otherwise, just chat up someone you like. If they don't know an answer, you've at least got to know a second WACKEN - Greenhorn, with which you can exchange your experiences.

Other things to keep in mind when making your preparations:

- Due to the high risk of cuts (sometimes festival visitors just fall into the botany for various reasons...) glass is FORBIDDEN on the whole area!!
- Access to the actual festival area is only permitted for persons with a valid ticket (there are both ticket and security checks at the entrances).
- Drinks and food may be taken along in unlimited quantity!
- Because of the cooling, not a few experienced festival visitors have decided to bring their own generators with them...

Note: these must be in perfect condition and consideration for other visitors is mandatory!

Author's note: these generators are quite loud and don't necessarily spread the best scent

- Tents and pavilions should be appropriate in size and number to the size of the group. For example: please do not sleep alone in a 6-person tent...there are over 75,000 other people who would like to find a place to sleep...
- your place to Camp is right next to your vehicle! Quiet fine...only

consequence: your vehicle, once parked, has to stay where it is!!!
- Vehicles over 7.5 tons must be registered in advance!

In addition to the camping ground, there are a few special areas that I don't want to withhold from you - even if this is part of the preparations for WACKEN 2020, because like everything else, first come, first served... So that you don't lose out, here are the preparations for the next preparations:

Special areas:

Additional or separate rules, privileges or restrictions apply here. According to the official WACKEN homepage these are the following:

Wheels of Steel Area:

This place is close to the stage area and will be kept free for Metalheads with handicaps and their companions. There are even skilled helpers who can repair broken equipment.

Author's note: that's one of the things I love so much about WACKEN: nobody is left behind there...

Camper Park WACKEN:

There are marked out plots here with electricity connection. The area tends to be quieter and more suitable for families than others...

Moshtel:

Container hotel located close to the stage. Since WACKEN does not have a hotel, hostel or similar, the organizers have fulfilled the wish of many fans for a permanent accommodation with the Moshtel, thus saving them the daily commute.
Author's note: in my opinion, commuting actually takes a lot of fun, even locals from Itzehoe were a bit annoyed last year because it wasn't so easy to get a bus after the final concert of the day...

Camping Only:

Directly next to the bus stop is the area where camping is only allowed without vehicles. It's quieter there because the otherwise typical large music systems are omitted.
Author's note: cool idea, but keep in mind that especially these music systems provide the special WACKEN-atmosphere, especially at night when the starry sky is as beautiful as last year.

World Metal Camp:

Together with the affiliated travel partners, the campers without their own vehicle will be provided with the necessary infrastructure for a successful festival. The focus there is on international exchange.
Author's note: definitely a great chance! Last year I was totally enthusiastic about the conversations with fans from all over the world and remember the especially lovingly group from Central America that saved their money for years to be able to go to WACKEN!

Full Metal Army Camp:

The fan-club organizes every year a big common camp with party tent, electricity and other conveniences...
Author's note: keep it as an outlook for the next years...

    There are also regulations for private tractors and for vehicles from 7.5 tons. Should this concern you contrary to expectations, please contact the organizers directly.

https://www.wacken.com/en/all-information/campground/

So, whoo, that was a lot of info.

My recommendation:

Lean back, mark the most important thing for you - hey, do you think I'm writing this book so that you treat it like a shrine? It only unfolds its effect with a little patina in the form of coffee stains, beer that has been knocked over and other smut.
Author's note: hey, enjoy your personal notes...which ever kind they might be

5 - MANY WAYS LEAD TO WACKEN

My path led me last year in a very relaxed way by train to WACKEN:
More precisely, to ITZEHOE.
I wasn't even aware how fast and direct it works, especially from the Ruhr area.
Therefor a clear recommendation on my part for this variant!
OK, of course it only works if the luggage is kept very tiny. To arrive with a huge suitcase in WACKEN might not be a good idea at all...on the other hand metalheads have a great sense of humor and you won't stay alone you're your luggage variant for long...

Great other advantages:

On the way, you can easily recognize other fans by the WACKEN T-shirt and if you like it, you can dock it and make contact. Especially when they have already been in WACKEN, you can get useful tips and e.g. when you arrive at the station ITZEHOE, you can relax and shackle behind them to make sure that you arrive at the shuttle bus.
I was more than enthusiastic about the organization on site: near the ITZEHOE railway station there is a small square with a sales stand for commuter tickets. These are valid for the entire duration of the festival and allow you to commute to Itzehoe, for example - if you

like it or have found accommodation there.

In 2018 the ticket costs have been 10 EUR – as far as I remember. At the bus station you can settle down and relax... I enjoyed sitting in the shade under the trees...I remember having bought some delicious cold beer there.

Contrary to all expectations, the metal fan waits completely relaxed for the regularly arriving shuttle buses to the festival area.

Pushing? No way!

On the contrary: everything is completely relaxed. It gets really funny on the bus. You'll probably be just as surprised as I am when you see what ingenious tools (2018 to survive the heat) other fans have on board.

I followed my heart and talked to the person sitting next to me pretty quickly. That was a great idea, because he outed himself as a New Zealander and our conversation made the trip very entertaining.

Since I came out as a total WACKEN-GREENHORN, other more experienced fans took care of me and took me under their wing.

In practical terms, this meant that a nice inhabitant of Itzehoe actually informed me about the most important procedures on the premises and thus made it easier for me to get started. In the end she was the reason why I am writing this book! Because not everyone experiences this grace, or is as uninhibitedly communicative as I am... With the help of this book I would like to give as many tips and information as possible to anyone who is not yet familiar with the subject, so that they can simply enjoy this ingenious festival!

By the way, the bus drops you off with all the other fans directly at the festival area (i.e. where everyone is camping without a vehicle). There are huge overview maps and the first view of the perceived infinity of the HOLY GROUND. I suppose that this is exactly when the feeling of great humility will spread to you...enjoy it! This is the spirit of the "first time". Inhale it, dive into it and give it a place in your heart forever!! It will never be like that again...ok, maybe it will be even better next year...

A real alternative seems to be the way of arriving, which I now report about:

Arrival with an official W:O:A travel partner:

This is for all those who wish to arrive as comfortable and pleasant as possible. The travel partners operate worldwide and offer not only a trip directly to the festival, but also exciting round trips (especially for fans from abroad). This also includes the legendary Metal Train, which I will certainly try out another year...

Take care to work together with the REAL travel partners, because they are Official Distributors and sell really valid tickets...unfortunately there are also people here who like to play the fool with ticket sales.

Find here the corresponding Internet pages with all further details:

https://www.mondialevents.de/

https://www.festicket.com/de/hosted/festivals/wacken-open-air/2019/

At Festticket.com there are some interesting offers for rental tents, Mondial offers shuttle services and support for accommodation incl. shuttle e.g. from Hamburg and Berlin.
Since the offers are very varied and of course quickly booked out, just have a look if you have need.

Because it is so ingenious, I enumerate here briefly the countries, for which the organizers have deposited individual information:

- Argentina
- Austria
- Belgium
- Brazil
- Colombia
- Costa Rica
- Denmark
- Ecuador
- Estonia
- Finland
- France (France)
- Germany
- Indian subcontinent
- Italy
- Luxembourg
- Mexico
- Netherlands
- Norway
- Russia
- Spain
- Sweden
- United Kingdom
- Uruguay
- Venezuela

By car, motorhome, motorbike and Co. to WACKEN:

Approach via motorways 7 and 23, the route is signposted according to the WACKEN homepage. Please turn off the navigation after the first signs, otherwise you will arrive at the wrong end of WACKEN!

If you follow the signs, you will end up at the signposts who will guide you to your place.

Very important:

It is not possible to choose a campsite yourself!
If you are part of a group and want to camp together with your buddies, make sure you arrive together and inform the staff. It is best to mark the vehicles that belong together conspicuously!

You should allow some time for check-in. Because it can be quite possible after current filling situation that you are led in waiting loops, in order to keep the most important traffic routes free for police, fire-brigade and the rescue service.

6 - FINALLY ON HOLY GROUND

Yahhh, you made it! You have actually arrived at Holy Ground WACKEN OPEN AIR for the first time!

Maybe you, just like me last year, take a little break and enjoy the vibes!

With a little luck the weather will be just as great this year and you can let your gaze wander over thousands of campers from the bus station, grasp the endless vastness and somewhere in the background recognize the stages with their huge superstructures...

This is true magic and appears in this rural environment like a mirage at first. First cope with it, then start exploring the scene!

You've arrived! In the next few days you will experience almost unbelievable experiences, you will walk over the ground with about 75,000 people, you will move enthusiastically from stage to stage, sing along, scream, jump, romp, laugh... in short: enjoy life to the full.

You still don't really know how touching these moments will be, you still haven't seen WACKEN at night, you haven't experienced what it feels like when thousands stand spellbound in front of the MAIN STAGE and listen to the music or sing along under the starry sky...one of the biggest and most vibrant choirs in the world...

Every year has its own unique atmosphere. Don't be deterred if the weather doesn't develop so well. Sometimes the waves are so high just because the world sinks into the rain and the feet in the mud. It doesn't matter at all: you don't have to maintain an artificial facade, you can be yourself, let yourself drift, live out your feelings - which may have been accumulated for some time - sinking into the sea of like-minded people who have gathered here, on HOLY GROUND, to celebrate this first days of August together.

Breathe! Feel! Enjoy!

So, now you can take the next step. One of many steps, because the terrain is truly huge: over 240 hectares of land lie in front of you...
You have no idea how much that is?
240 hectares correspond to 2,4km², for football fans: at the highest allowed football field according to the rules (90 x 120m) 240 hectares correspond to 240 football fields!

If you rather think in m²: 1 hectare corresponds to 10.000 m², that means, WACKEN OPEN AIR has 2.400.000 m² ...in words 2,4 million square meters!!!

It's definitely worth buckling up your pedometer. I think, even with a minimal radius of movement with many beer breaks, a lot of distance travelled comes together!

Orientation is therefore THE keyword and enormously important during your stay in WACKEN. After all, you want to see the concerts that are closest to your heart and it is very helpful if you can calculate the time you need to get there and, above all, if you know where your path should take you....

Remember: if you approach from the campground, you have to go through the security barrier every time before you arrive at the

INFIELD, the actual HOLY GROUND.
The organizers are of course aware of this challenge, so they have done everything to make your orientation easier.

There are huge posters right next to the bus station showing the area with all the stages, facilities and event times. I took a few photos of them myself, but you can also download the WACKEN-APP specially designed for this festival.

https://www.wacken.com/en/all-information/app/

So, it is time to explain the individual areas to you in more detail:

The INFIELD - THE HOLY LAND

Here are the biggest stages of the festival. Particularly impressive is the huge double stage FASTER & HARDER, which is visible from afar and flanked by the round arch stage LOUDER.

These three stages are the venue for the festival's biggest and most elaborate concerts. Especially in the evening, when the stage shows really come into their own, an absolute MUST.

This is the place! The artists are allowed to get involved beforehand and it is not unusual that the two stages FASTER and HARDER are combined for a stage show. Whole symphony orchestras have space here and have already performed there.

The alternating use of the three stages makes it possible to keep the rebuilding breaks quite short.

During normal stage operation, FASTER and HARDER are each played by a different band, while the LOUDER stage is being rebuilt. After that the stage will be changed.

To prevent everything from sinking into the mud in bad weather, an extensive drainage system has been installed there.

In addition, the world-famous beer pipeline ensures that

everything inside remains beautifully smooth and drying times are avoided.

WACKEN CENTER

On your way to the HOLY GROUND you will pass by the WACKEN CENTER. There's the BEERGARDEN - Stage, idyllically situated in a beer garden with seating and plenty of beer. At the beginning of the festival, the WACKEN volunteer fire brigade's music procession performs right there. Unfortunately I missed it last year, so this year it's on my ToDo, or rather ToEnjoy list.

Next to the stage there is a video wall, where every year some movies are shown... and that gives me one more point for my ToEnjoy

Had you thought so: there is also a metal market here where you can go shopping in peace between the concerts. Numerous stalls offer everything around Metal, including very special things you won't find at other locations. It's definitely worth to drop by!
Close by is the WACKEN FOUNDATION CAMP where some non-profit organizations have their booths. Definitely worth a visit.
RAINBOW - bar, various food stands, sanitary facilities and ATMs complete the scene.

WACKEN VILLAGE & WASTELAND

This is the other side of WACKEN...here it is really exciting: Medieval dressed people, MET at the bar (Author's note: amazingly tasty!!!). - Last year I enjoyed the Met booth while listening to all the other bands on stage and at the same time got wet directly from the roof because of the heat.)

Culinary specialties, bagpipers next to cage fighters, a flame show...here you will find everything medieval fans could wish for.

These are located on the southern side of the terrain. On the stage of the WACKINGER STAGE installed there are medieval rock, pagan metal
Author's note: whatever that is...I'll watch it this year
and folk (which last year was really fun with mead in my hand and made the audience jump for joy despite 30°C).

If you prefer to step into the future in the southern half of the Village instead of the past, you're place to be is in the northern half of the VILLAGE: in WASTELAND.

Ok, that's not one of my favorites, but that doesn't mean that it's not YOURS...here's the Post-Apocalypse, with the WASTELAND WARRIORS and their crazy outfits and of course lots of shows and other activities.

Special highlight: the WASTED WEDNESDAY...ok, I wasn't there yet, so again something for this year's ToEnjoy list!!!

WACKEN PLAZA

I often and extensively stayed there last year because of the nearby toilets and showers, as well as my favorite, the lockers with electricity connection!!! To my opinion one of the best meeting places, because everyone who wants to store their valuables safely gathers there. It's a leisurely place where you can rest, load your mobile phone, change your clothes and have a nice chat with others. I will go into this in more detail in one of the following chapters.

In the middle of the PLAZA, the WELCOME TO THE JUNGLE location attracts with its snugly PARAGU-stage, roofed seating (nice in any weather) and a kind of quiet zone in the vibrating WACKEN. Here all the small but fine performances like the SPOKEN WORD gigs take place...

The BULLHEAD CITY CIRCUS is really fun. This huge tent is awesome!

The two stages W.E.T. and HEADBANGER STAGE are not bound to certain genres and are always exciting. Especially because during the day they have the possibility to score with crazy stage shows.

THE night of the nights takes place here on Thursday evening, the NIGHT TO DISMEMBER.

It was on everyone's lips last year! I also liked to dive into these tents again and again.

CAMP SITES

Well, and then there are of course the camping sites, which I will only mention briefly here, as I mentioned these in Chapter 4 more detail already.

- CAMPING GROUND
For traveler with vehicles up to 7.5 tons without prior notice

- CAMPER-PARK-WACKEN
Plots with electricity, suitable for families, quieter

- MOSTEL
Container Hotel, close to the stage area, permanent accommodation

- CAMPING-ONLY
Camping grounds for all those who have arrived without a vehicle

- WORLD-METAL-CAMP
Camping area for fans without a vehicle who have travelled with the official travel partners.

- FULL METAL ARMY CAMP

Camp organized by the WACKEN OPEN AIR Fanclub with party tent, electricity and many extras.

Author's note: this is for the advanced, so here is just a preview

WACKEN AND SURROUNDINGS

In the meantime, not only the original village of WACKEN has been integrated into the festival, but also the surrounding villages and communities that are close by: Gribbohm, Bokelrehm and Holstenniendorf, as well as Besdorf and Vaale.

Author's note: for people who didn't grow up in this area, like me, these place names are part of the WACKEN-FLAIRS...because they are so special.

The village WACKEN itself is described in more detail in Chapter 15, because it definitely deserves its own chapter!

METAL CHURCH

THE hip and extraordinary concert location during the festival or better said: in the run-up to the festival... That's why I haven't seen it live yet, but heard from many visitors last year that it's a real MUST for every fan. Therefor definitely something to add to my ToEnjoy – List this year!

A few very special events will take place there on a small scale with specially selected artists. I already get goose bumps while writing! The price is included in the ticket price, probably it is not so easy to be able to step in there, because admission is limited.

That's why you can spend unforgettable hours there in a small but nice atmosphere.

This is the place to meet experienced visitors, some of whom have been loyal to WACKEN for decades!

7 - CARE - PACKAGE

Now it's getting serious! It's on the ground.
In the first place you have to find the real entrance area... not that easy the first time, because the way from the bus station to WACKEN PLAZA is already an adventure on its own... Yes, you can also enter from the village WACKEN, but I just assume now that you have arrived with the bus shuttle or already settled on the camping ground.

In 2018 I was very grateful that my dear companion accompanied me until almost before the issue of the ribbons, because I confess: I could hardly have done it alone.

The way there, past thousands and thousands of camping fans, was already an experience in itself! With all the dust and the heat with temperatures more than 30°C already a real challenge.

Despite all the instruction and all the advice I would not have found the ribbon edition area on my own and had to ask shortly before again.

To have the ticket validated and the festival ribbon (a sanctuary that I still proudly wear after one year) handed to me with the care package should be one of your first actions, because you are safe after that and check the rest in peace.

Ticket sales besides those by official agencies like the advance sale at WACKEN OFFICIAL or the affiliated travel partners are extremely tricky by the way!

Passing them on in the circle of friends or family is of course no problem, but don't buy them from anyone other than those mentioned above! If, despite all warnings, you have come across someone who has sold you illegal and therefore invalid tickets, please go and immediately report this to the police!

Only two types of tickets are available:

X-MAS-TICKET

A limited ticket that costs 10 EUR less than the regular ticket and includes a free t-shirt as an extra. It is limited to 10.000 pieces and I can only mention according to my experience that it is not easy to get one. I've been waiting in front of the PC for some time last year to get one, but: no chance...I haven't even seen it show up on the screen yet...

3-DAYS-ALL-IN-TICKET

This is the normal regular ticket that most people call their own. It is limited to 65,000 pieces.

All other tickets like VIP tickets, day tickets, group tickets or similar are simply bullshit!

What is included in your ticket?

(according to official information at www.wacken.com)

- Camping at no extra cost from Monday, 29.07.2019
- Camping directly at the car
- Free use of all showers and toilets
- Live music from Wednesday, 31.07.2019 up to and including Saturday, 03.08.2019
- Over 150 acts on 8 stages
- Extensive supporting program with main topics such as the Middle Ages and the Last Days

For safety's sake:

The most important rules at a glance

- Common sense and consideration for other visitors, artists and employees.
- Glass is forbidden everywhere due to the high risk of cuts.
- You can take an unlimited amount of food and drinks with you on the camping site.
- Grilling and cooking is allowed on the campsites with coal, electricity and gas.
- Open fires are prohibited, including fire baskets and the like.
- Power generators are permitted to a limited extent
- When using power generators, music systems and similar equipment, care must be taken that neighbors are not unduly

disturbed.
- All devices and objects such as generators, refrigerators, gas bottles, grills and the like may only be used if they are in a technically perfect condition.
- Weapons are forbidden on the whole area. Tools, eating knives and the like may only be used on stage.
- Large bags and backpacks are forbidden on the stage area!
So and if you are wondering how you can take your most important things with you when bags and backpacks are not allowed on the inner stage area (and believe me, you will be checked!) then we are now on a topic that is not mentioned much on the official site: the care package.

Last year I was both surprised and enthusiastic about what I found in it...

Content Care Package 2018:

- A small mini backpack, more like a pouch that you can hang on your back - or in front of your stomach, if you are afraid that somebody might steal from you...
- Earplugs...didn't need them, or later on another occasion. They are really great and can be used by the bands as ear protection as

well as at night for sleeping.
- Throat tablets - I tested them much later on other occasions. Through constant voice lubrication with the tasty beers on the festival grounds, my vocal survived.
- A Wackenwurst! Mega delicious, I have carried so to speak quite fast in the firmly built in backpack of my body...wants to say: my stomach.

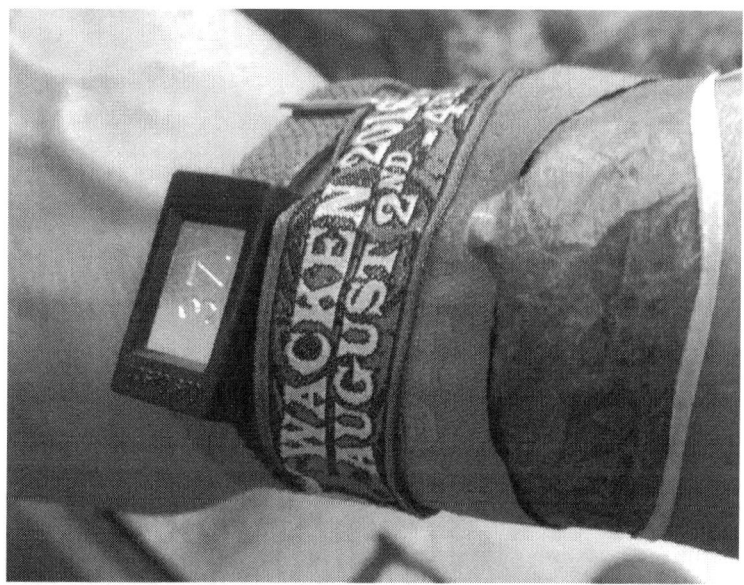

- The drinking bottle is also totally ingenious! An absolute must, because from time to time pure water is not to be despised. The good one is constructed like a bag, therefore foldable and equipped with a closable drinking cap. I have refilled it again and again in the shower or toilet facilities. Absolutely necessary for survival in the heat of last year.
- A rain cape (last year it was not used, I used it then also on other occasion)
- Condoms (yes, the organizers have really thought of everything)
- Then there was a little bag to tie up, or was it for the wrist? That

was missing with me unfortunately... I hope in this connection on this year!

- I can still remember matches, and the rest of the memory has somehow gone under in the heat...

- Well, just let yourself be surprised of the content of your bag this year!!!

8 - CLOSING FACILITIES WITH CIRCUIT AND OTHER THINGS TO MENTION

One of my favorite places last year have actually been at the lockers! Yes, I was so flashed that on the one hand there was something as ingenious as these lockers and even more enthusiastic that these lockers had what we never got at the fairs: they do have sockets!!! This may sound ridiculous, but most of us are not able to survive without charging our mobile phones.

My son had kindly given me a separate battery, so I could charge the battery or the mobile phone alternately....

And by the way, I could always make exciting contacts, hang out a little, sort my stuff and think about my plans for the future.

I had the best conversations right here:
With the young chief of a bakery, who told me at three in the morning how he had prepared for his WACKEN and that his sister had provided him with the money for the appropriate equipment: sturdy shoes, T-shirt, clothes... everything you need in WACKEN.

He also advised me not to always hang out with my buddies, but above all to devote myself to personal music, because WACKEN simply offers the unique opportunity to do so.

Then came the question that I've never forgotten since: Who is your band, your music here on WACKEN?

I confess, I had no immediate answer because I was totally unprepared and definitely most of the bands were totally unknown by me...

You can't imagine how horrified his face looked like! "What, you're here on WACKEN and can't tell me what YOUR music is? Which band does YOUR heart beat for? What kind of music do you love the most to listen to?"

He was absolutely stunned, because for him the music style simply decided everything... In retrospect I agree with him, because there is a very big difference whether your heart beats for Romantic songs (ok, it's unlikely that you will like these if you read this book - but you never know...) or for Metal or f.e. for the end-time mood... That tells of course a lot about you, about your character, your attitude to life and also about the people you like to surround yourself with and the places where you feel comfortable...

Well, this year, WACKEN 2019, I can answer his question: My heart beats for the Sisters of Mercy: and MY favorite song is "MORE" . This year I will be as close to the stage as possible and sing along as loud as I can...

What is YOUR song? YOUR band? See you at the stage??? Or rather at the lockers? By the way, there are two stations lockers, one at the WACKEN PLAZA, just before the entrance to the HOLY GROUND and then again near the CAMPING GROUND at the second main entrance to the stages. Pretty cool because you can lock your valuables there before the next concert starts and don't have to burden yourself unnecessarily with luggage - which is not allowed anyway. Believe me, you will soon be very grateful for it.

We owe the lockers to a Berlin startup - the BigBoxBerlin!

They are looked after and monitored day and night by staff. They are available in two sizes and with 15W or 90W maximum socket power.
Here is the link to the locker:

https://festivalsafeboxen.bigboxberlin.de/festivals/wacken-open-air/

I was lucky last year, but it's better to book them online before the festival!!!
I already own one...

Something else that is very exciting is the POSTSTATION on the WACKEN PLAZA, right next to the lockers. Yes, you got me! It is an absolute MUST to send a card home from there with your own WACKEN stamps.

Even if there are usually long queues, don't miss it!

9 – FOLLOW THE VIBES

Yeah, that's the best tip I can give you on the way! Follow the VIBES! No matter what is on your plan: LIFE takes place exactly when we make plans... and simply puts a stop to our calculations.

Yes, of course it makes sense to make a rough plan, but just as the officially announced stand isn't always the best at trade fairs, there are also moments in WACKEN that are MUCH better than anything you've planned before.

I may have already told you that I get myself in the mood every day by watching and listening to the official WACKEN-trailer. Today I discovered a new detail! Yes, our subconscious only shows us what we want to focus on or what we want to see.

What did I discover today? I watched with glittering eyes the scene in which the fan in the turtleneck was lifted above all heads! Isn't that gorgeous?

Here not only nobody is left behind, but much better: everyone is taken along!

Besides, I followed my main vibe and (several times each day !!!!) I got a lot of fun watching the brilliant video of "Within Temptation - Faster", the music that carries the second part of the WACKEN trailer and motivates me every day to finish and publish this book at the right time.

Here's the place where I ask YOU once again: "What is YOUR music this year, YOUR best experience, THE encounter that brings YOU tears of emotion and joy into your eyes?"

If you can't make a statement so far, then "FOLLOW YOUR VIBES". "Okay," you might be wondering, "What does she mean?" Well, just let yourself drift!

If you take a little time, you will notice that there are always streams of visitors in WACKEN. Be it that they walk towards the CAMPING GROUND to get ready for the evening concerts after a meal together, be it that there's one of THE gigs on the HARDER+FASTER+LOUDER stages right now, or there's a lot of people moving into the tent... or to one of the many beer stands... or just to the VILLAGE or the swimming pool... whatever, get involved, develop a new sensitivity for the VIBES that are in the air...and I tell you, there are a lot of Vibes...so follow the ones that trigger you...no matter what dates you've already made.
It's worth it!

If you like, write me and I will report your experiences next year as an inspiration for WACKEN 2020!
I already know that I will see WIHTIN FASTER in a few weeks... oh, nonsense, a few days, in any case, from whose song I am already totally enthusiastically now! This is going to be great!
Will we see each other there???

10 - INCOMING CONTROLS

Very important: always plan enough time for the admission controls!
Where do these take place? Whenever you stroll from the outside area, the VILLAGE or the CAMPING GROUND back to the actual festival area, you will be checked through!

Please note that you must

- DO NOT take large bags or backpacks with you (if in doubt, put them in the locker, as they are very close to the entrances, also for this reason).
- It is also NOT allowed to take food and drinks with you to the INNER GROUND! You can take them to the CAMPING GROUND, but not to the concerts. The only thing you can take with you is the foldable bottle which is included in the care package. This can be easily refilled with drinking water at all water points (usually near the toilet facilities). This can also be very useful as a supplement to beer when the heat is lower than 2018.
- Oh yes, glass is of course also forbidden because of the risk of injury, but you already know that...

- Any tools (ok, what should you do with them in the INNER GROUND????) and eating knives are also forbidden on the HOLY GROUND.

Well, even though you might be complaining now, these safety checks and clear rules are a major factor in making a festival of this gigantic size (you remember: 75,000 paying visitors on 2.4 million square meters) so wonderfully peaceful.

By the way, the controls are separated into men and women because of the final body search. This is often an advantage in terms of time ... if you belong to the females...

11 - OUTFIT

Fine feathers make fine birds- being in WACKEN most feathers are black, light black, dark black...

If your preparations for WACKEN have been farsighted, I am sure you additionally bought THE WACKEN T-Shirt 2019. That solves most of your clothing problems. Congratulations!

If somebody might spill beer on your sanctuary (yes, it will be one from now on, because thanks to the care package you can apply your stickers and spice it up according to your mood) it might make sense to add more T-shirts to your luggage.

Maybe you belong to a bigger group and you have had your own t-shirts made for WACKEN.

Otherwise: tattoos, lots of naked skin, leather, hot fishnet pantyhose and short minis for the women, wild hair, leather vests, rivets, boots for the men...there are no limits to your imagination.

Especially if you are one of the fans of WASTELAND or a MITTELAGE fan. If you, because it is your first time, are not yet perfectly prepared, no problem. Maybe even better, because it then makes sense to go shopping at the METALTIX-SHOP in the village or at the numerous sales stands within the STAGE AREA and choose the right one for you... and above all: it has gotten the same dust as you and is really wrapped up...

Yeahh, last year I also bought myself a correspondingly cheerful black T-shirt, on which I ironed my WACKEN EMBLEM and which of course will be on the site again this year.

If you still need a few suggestions: have a look here in the WACKEN-GALLERY:

http://gallery.wacken.com/

12 - LIFE ON THE MEADOW

With reference to WACKEN 2018, this meant sweating in the endless expanses of land used for agricultural purposes during the rest of the year, which now dried out and spread out to the horizon in dusty conditions, wandering around on the endless, mostly black-clad, figures, lying somewhere in the shade, sitting together for breakfast, simply hanging out, letting one's soul dangle, or giving oneself entirely to the music from the boxes one brought along.
The most frequently asked question has been:

"What's worse? - The mud 2017 or the dust 2018"?

The latter had in any case the consequence that most visitors crept rather slowly over the meadow and a small midday nap was quite announced.
The ones in better condition sat either comfortably in their small tent town, often on beer crates, or had made themselves comfortable in the shade of the food stalls with a tasty beer.

Since I was alone on the way, I could simply let myself drift. I can only recommend anyone who - like me - doesn't have the circle of friends and acquaintances to go with him to WACKEN - to simply drive alone.

Because: You are not really alone! No matter where you stand or sit, be sure, if you like, you will get into conversation!

WACKEN has an absolutely familiar atmosphere! Yes, there are indeed some old WACKEN - visitors who arrive completely with Family. As already described, there is, for example, the CAMPER-PARK-WACKEN, where things are a little quieter. While on the second day I was bathing my already damaged feet in the soft sand of a food supply island, I had a funny conversation going on with a family sitting next to me. They had simply rented a camper van for the WACKEN days. Probably calculating in that the final cleaning for this trip would be a bit more expensive. But what the hell?

Not having my own retreat surely has been one of my biggest personal challenges. My luggage and sleeping bag just fitted into one of the largest lockers available. If I had only had a few more things with me, things would have been difficult, because your are nearly allowed to take anything into the INNER AREA.

My small locker was not only the place to go to recharge my mobile phone, but also to have a nice chat with the fans from all over the world. It wasn't unusual at all to meet one's own locker neighbors several times a day and have a short chat about all the experiences you have made and of course about all that was still going on.

These conversations helped me to refine my stage plans and to visit tents and locations that I hadn't noticed before.

There was only one thing I could not do: to secure a place to sleep. Although I found a small shop in the village where you could buy all the tent equipment for very little money, I didn't feel like burdening myself with it. Especially because I remembered all too well from earlier holidays that such a small tent offers neither particularly good protection against noise nor heat.

Admittedly, I was a little stressed because somewhere in the back of my head there was always the question: "where am I staying tonight?"

Well, first of all, in the stream of visitors walking home from the last official concert on the main stage, I met a fan who even came from my neighborhood, namely from Düsseldorf.

He was also on his own, as he had been invited with a buddy for business reasons. But that buddy had gotten lost - that happened sometimes.

Since he had a good connection to the organizers and we still wanted to chat a little, he took me with him to the VIP area.

At this late (early) hour there wasn't much going on there either. To say nothing of the wild and excessive life of the bands...it was all very set and there was not so much to eat and drink anymore.

As an interior designer I was of course very interested in how this area was designed. I confess it didn't impress me too much.

And to put it bluntly between you and me: to wait for 6 hours on one of the stakes to get the permission to visit the VIP-Area? - No thanks!!! Rather celebrate properly with normal visitors, because that's definitely more fun over there.

Around three in the morning we parted ways again and I returned, meanwhile already quite tired (hadn't slept for 24 hours besides all the excitement) to my locker and had the super nice conversation with the master baker about music and the motivation and mercy to visit this festival.

Yes, I could have asked if I could spend the night with him in the group, but something stopped me.

Well, the time had come to look for a nice place to get some restful sleep.

Shouldn't be a problem, because of course there was enough meadow. The meadow in combination with a high number of beer-loving men offered and probably bestows a small challenge even this year:

The challenge to recognize if there are any places in which the common man does not release his beer in slightly modified consistence out of his body in the middle of the night.

Devastating result of my field research: there is actually NO place, because most men don't like to go too far away from their tents, camper vans or similar accommodations at night and can act relatively flexible due to the very own, very user-friendly built-in drainage system... means: (in the worst case for me): Open the door, open the fountain....

Conclusion for me: poor prospects...

Next thought: Men love their cars, so doesn't it make sense to simply lie down between two particularly chic vehicles, because men will never empty themselves...

Ooh Shit they will!!! Men, you are simply unrestrained!
Why can I be so sure? Well, I had the pleasure to be in the right place at the right time... or so to say: I was forced to watch it.

My gut feeling fortunately kept me from really lying between two parked cars. Instead, the good advice of my companion from the very beginning of my festival visit appeared to me: "just lie under an awning if you don't know what to do."

Relatively close to my location there was actually a snugly looking, old motorhome with a canopy. At these temperatures completely sufficient.
As fate would have it, however, (**Murphy's Law**) just when I had made myself comfortable on the ground (ok, comfortable is different, because a dust-dry ground is rock-hard) the door of the motorhome opened and the inhabitant stepped outside.

"Shit", has been my first thought... but it was not bad at all, because he was really cute!!

In the first place he looked at me, totally worried that I really planned to sleep all alone outside on the naked floor and then he invited me to his, certainly more comfortable, bedroom and even offered a coffee. After he confessed that there was only one bed, I thankfully refused. However, now I was officially allowed to sleep under his awning.

Now it got funny because exactly after our conversation he told me that he has to go peeing and placed himself exactly between the two cars where I was wondering short time ago to spend my night...

Ok girls: If you are homeless in WACKEN...take my advice: Check out the nearest canopy... homeless also means that you are not able to locate your tent in the middle at the night, that your tent is way too far to reach in your present condition or that you fell out with your buddies...

Stay brave, I am sure, you find a solution!

Otherwise: enjoy the views of all the fantastically imaginative arrangements and overnight accommodations that the others have created! From perfectly styled caravans with the WACKEN logo to wonderfully improvised old companions, there's practically everything.

Next year everything will be better, don't lose courage, after all, it would be a pity if you couldn't improve!!

For my part, I don't feel like spending the night on the hard floor again this year and I will also take a lot more time to get there. After all, the most touching concerts already take place before the actual festival! Just now I am in the process of transforming my already

existing trailer into a snug WACKEN-QUARTER, which in case of doubt offers me protection even during heavy rain (do you remember 2017?). Such a little nap every now and then can't hurt either, so that I'm fit and rested for the really awesome gigs.
(as far as that's possible in WACKEN...)

13 - TOILETS & SHOWERS

For many, certainly a horror topic or at least a horror performance...doesn't have to be: You are at WACKEN after all!

And for that reason, please consider that: The toilets are unisex! At least in the large areas of the CAMPING GROUND or better said the WACKEN PLAZA. There is a large area right next to the post office and at the other main entrance to the INFIELD next to the lockers.

It is always a good idea to come outside the most frequently common times. Last year it was even relatively crowded in the morning. This may have been because it was extremely hot and you couldn't stand it for long in the tent.

But even if there should be a waiting queue: don't despair! On the one hand, this is always a good chance to get into conversation with other Metals you didn't know before, on the other hand, everything usually takes place quietly and peacefully.

By the way, the actual toilet block is divided into different areas so that you only wait as long as necessary:

- On the one hand, there is an area very close to the post office that is only intended for (hand) washing. It's similar to the washing troughs that you may have come across during your stay in a youth hostel. Easy to handle and of course very communicative.

- The "most waiting-intensive" areas are, as you can guess, the toilets. They are arranged in several lines (at least that's how it has been like in 2018)
- You can find Showers in a separate area. It They are build open as a huge space, no small private cabins! Finally, according to the washbasins: a long series of showers installed above wooden planks, so you are sure to be safe and don't have to bath your feed in the mud.

Don't worry: they are separated into male and female!

In the HOLY GROUND there are different toilet facilities, not far away from the stages of the MAINSTAGES. They are built as usual, like small container wagons with toilets. Not exactly luxurious, but ok!

Well, you certainly didn't expect Luxury either. The toilets in the VIP area are a bit nicer... but not necessarily as much better as that (in my inconsequential opinion) sitting out on the stakes for 6 hours would be worth it... unless you love to just sit up there and enjoy the view anyway.

In case you are a little "lost":

In case of doubt always follow the signs! For instance the huge posters with all concert details and other information and: just ask anybody, because quite a lot of other festival visitors know where to go.

One more thing: Close to the WACKEN PLAZA there are additionally placed "popular" Dixies. The lines over there are usually shorter, because to use them is quite unpleasant most of the time...

Your choice!!!

14 – FOOD & DRINKS

The same applies here as for the other areas: Don't you worry, everything is taken care of!

Please keep some basic distinctions in mind:

- Eating + drinking on the CAMPING GROUND is totally easy and relaxed: You simply bring what you need and like to have at your disposal. This is definitely the cheapest option. When you need supplies, it's always a great idea to go to the village. On the one hand you support the residents who make this great event possible, on the other hand it is the closest possibility to get something - and above all the funniest! Once you've walked through the village, you'll see that the positive and open atmosphere often shown in the media actually prevails everywhere! Last year, for example, I went to the village for breakfast (at a perfect low price since I had breakfast directly with the locals) and was able to observe how many people already know each other through constant WACKEN visits. It is very common to listen to a conversation like this: "Hey, how nice that you are here again! It's already how many years you come here?" I am sure that many lasting friendships have already developed here.

- In addition, there are some stands at the CAMPING GROUND that offer breakfast, for example, nice in the shade or dry - depending on the weather. A little chat with other guests you may not know yet, inclusive.

- Food and Drinks in the Village: Many villagers use the time to improve their household budget. There are beer tents on the doorstep, children with their grandmothers or parents selling homemade food, shops with special offers during the WACKEN days... beer stands, cocktail bars and all kinds of offers. I recommend to enjoy as many visits to the village and its inhabitants as possible!

I can only recommend to enjoy your Food + Drinks on WACKEN PLAZA.

Advantage:

No security check all time. It's ideal in "the-hours-in-between" when your timetable offers you a few moments, to relax a bit and take it easy without having to cook for yourself. Just check all the international meals. But hey, just give them a try next year when you're back.

EAT + DRINK on the HOLY GROUND. Well, you won't starve in there either. Maybe you prefer to drift from band to band and don't want to commute to your tent, caravan or similar in between. Besides the countless possibilities to have a well-groomed drink, there are at least as many opportunities to consume tasty food. There are particularly exciting things to see at the medieval markets. Last year I drank MET for the first time, admittedly mainly because I wanted to stay at the stand within the heat of the day, furthermore a band performed on the nearby stage... Soo tasty! I will definitely do it again this year...

If you like, place a comment about THE food or drink stand that has been your favorite this year. Then I can pass it on to all new Beginners next year!

15 – THE VILLAGE

An absolute recommendation for every beginner is a visit to the village WACKEN. The way is not quite so short, but manageable. Supplementary there is a bus shuttle to the village, which starts at the bus station you already know. The **W:O:A Pool Shuttles** will run several times a day from Tuesday, 30.07.2019. Further information can be found directly at the bus station, which is closely connected to the festival area and at www.wacken.com

If you prefer to walk comfortably into the village, it's best to choose the exit to the bus station directly from the INNER GROUND. If you're lucky (or if you ask someone who knows their way around) you'll find the path that turns left before the actual bus station and leads you directly to the exit in the direction of the village.

I almost start to rave when I think of my first "walk to the VILLAGE" last year. Yes, I admit, I had to ask someone first... That's definitely worth it, because strolling along WACKEN's main street during festival times is a real pleasure.

Everywhere you see happily black dressed people who have fun together, also strolling along the main street or already settled down in one of the "Places-to-be" on the right and left side of the street.

Anyone who has decided to move from one beer stand to the next and try some of the local specialties in between, has set themselves some goals!

Countless stands, stalls and pavilions are available, some run by locals, some by travelling merchants. Making a decision is a real challenge. Just don't think too much about it - hey, you're in WACKEN and just want to have fun. My experience has been that no matter which stand you choose, the decision is always a good one because it's totally nice and of course refreshing and delicious everywhere.

For all those who need more than just something to eat or drink, or have already enjoyed too much of the drinks, there is the **Duhorn Pharmacy!** This is also a good place to go for all those who may suffer from diabetes, have injured themselves against expectations or otherwise feeling a little sick.

The **HANGOVER WACKEN** offers similar solutions... probably less suitable for diabetics, but certainly a good alternative for the "hard Ones", who simply keep going, even if the skull is booming.

Who would have thought that: if you can't tolerate gluten, for example, you're in good hands there. In case of doubt just ask! You will surely be helped!

Freshly strengthened for a little shopping? No problem: the **W:O:A OUTLETSTORE** is not far away. Remaining goods and rarities to a special price are always present, the normal merchandise-articles naturally too. Furthermore, as already mentioned, you can ask at the helpdesk for everything that moves you or what you haven't found yet.

Expert talks among fans are of course always inclusive.

After shopping its time for a little break again...You can enjoy it in the classic beer garden atmosphere in the **"Landgasthof zur Post"**.

Freshly tapped beer cools particularly well at heat and freshly prepared meals are also available.

The huge sign that adorns the balcony above the entrance area also brightens the mood: "be happy, you are in WACKEN" I think that you don't have to recommend this again to most people here, because I can't actually remember anyone who wasn't happy to be in WACKEN. We all took a lot on ourselves, starting with the annual hunt for the highly coveted tickets.

By the way: if you still have friends with you who have been dawdling and therefore don't own any tickets yet, you have a good chance of getting some on the main street.

Since I couldn't find a fellow traveler last year, I resold my second ticket to make someone else happy. Basically, the sale of tickets is not very popular (and officially forbidden), because there are, as far too often, some black sheep who try to make a quick profit with illegal tickets...

Prices are a matter of negotiation. My experience: the more advanced the festival is, the less will be paid for a card. Absolutely sensible, because if the price paid is always below the normal price of the tickets, it definitely doesn't make sense for people who want to bunker tickets and then resell them at horrendous prices!

Before I get to the other exciting locations, a little note about the "outfit" of the village: Don't be surprised that many residents have secured their properties with construction site fences. They surely have good reasons for this, because some "slightly drunken" WACKEN-FAN has probably already made a mistake in the address, or not noticed much and therefore behaved quite undue.
The advantage of the building fences is besides clearly the fact that one can attach so great posters to them!
To put myself back in the vibes of the last year, I am browsing through the photos I took last year with my mobile phone on my second monitor.
One photo shows a really ingenious poster that reads: "HÖLLENSCHISS - burns twice. Since 2008. Shots 1EUR."

The pictograms you look at the best on the inserted photo itself, that is better than to describe them here elaborately ...

Great idea is the setting up of a "deposit -goal-wall". As you can see on the photo, the house owner has come up with something very special: a sign with the inscription "deposit" shows you where you can throw your cans. Each hit counts and the local resident later has his fun with the deposit. A real win-win situation...like almost always in WACKEN.

A good orientation on the way is the well visible **WACKEN-TOWER** with a lot of mobile phone masts, which ensure us to post nice photos... Even better will be the reports of the NDR, which also positioned its OB truck nearby. If you're looking for a career as an actor, singer or TV star, check them out... Who knows, maybe it'll be "love at first sight" and WACKEN will change your future life even more than you've ever imagined.

It is nice to find a shady place to rest along the way: just sit on the sidewalk, done. You probably won't be sitting alone for long.

Especially not if you put a stuffed animal on the street in front of you, preferably plus a collecting cup. You're already in conversation with people strolling by! Humor is always a solution in WACKEN!

There's no lack of advertising, the posters just look different than usual! The "played joke" was one of last year's posters that said: "Well, are you freezing?". Hahaaahh, nobody was freezing not even at night! That's why the suggestion to book a holiday was probably not very attractive for most people. This might have changed always certainly "after WACKEN", especially because in this case the offering has been a "full metal holiday".

The prices in the village are also unbeatable: at the **OeTTI** meeting "supervised drinking" directly at the tower, the offer has been 0.5 l cold beer for 1.50 EUR, draft beer at 2.50 EUR. You really can't complain about that...so order one, but rather quickly!

When your gaze wanders upwards and your eyes meet with the information of a sign: "Welcome Metalheads! Be happy you are in WACKEN", the beers and all the other little pints taste even better!

The **"Eddelaker Baumstriezel"**, which was offered at a cute little wooden crispy house near the path, looked very tasty. Definitely another treat for my "ToEnjyo list" this year!

For the less discerning gourmets there are of course the absolute BASICS on offer: French fries, grilled sausage, curry sausage and neck steaks...at really fair prices.

If the stomach is satisfied, the palate might want to enjoy another delicacy: barrel beer was charged at relaxed 1.50 EUR and you could get a sunny cocktail for 4.00 EUR.

Enjoy walking HAPPY-go-LUCKY through the village.
A lot of families put all their energy into it every year and spontaneously turn their garden into a small beer garden with a cocktail counter. Meet other groups of people at these snugly places, for whom WACKEN is a fixed part of the year's program. Beginners are lovingly integrated and entertained with stories from past years. Just go for it!

If you're missing something, there's a shop, which sells tents, chairs, rubber boots, small paddling pools, sleeping bags and so. Opened from Wednesday, so that no WACKEN fan who's rashly driven off has to miss his favoured equipment. Always at low prices.

Several hotspots in WACKEN provide you with enjoying WLAN. There's also a stylish black and white giant screen with all the details, including instructions on how to set it up. Rarely has anyone cared so lovingly and clearly about my daily needs. Just try it out.

If the poster is not black, but like this photo YELLOW, you should pay special attention to it! "We love our Neighbors! Please respect them. They make this possible!" is a hint that you should follow in order to keep this festival so wonderfully cheerful and peaceful.

Other posters communicate deep wisdom: "Whoever swings has more of the way" is definitely one of them.

The **"ManaMana-Bar"** offers help:
on the one hand you can enjoy the special offers of the "Happy Hell's Fuck Hour", in which the fiery drink is sold per meter. As if that weren't enough, the bar also offers a liquid breakfast: ideal for all those for whom chewing has become too much after all the exertion.

If you are no longer able to stand the whole hellish spectacle you can retire to the venerable church of the village. Idyllically situated near the park, this is a place that I will definitely visit this year.

Very refreshing was the garden of another, very special WACKEN resident: on the one hand his chic old Deutz tractor was for sale and on the other hand he had come up with something special for cooling down, to which he pointed out with a handwritten sign the following wording: "Please, free cooling down please!"

As a beginner, I was somewhat perplexed as to what the cooling should consist of. Only a rather large green plastic bowl and a watering can could be seen.

Fortunately, the inventor of this cooling hurried out of his house when he saw my helpless look. The thing was as simple as it was effective: Take the watering can, fill it with ice-cold water and pour it over your neck, face or whatever you like. It was nice to be helped and the "Master himself" refreshed my heated mind! Soo nice and definitely worth a big THANK YOU.

What else is there? Well, the "Old Metal Bar Wacken" for example. Hard to overlook, because a white skeleton with a feathered hat on the side of the road points to it decoratively and gave its best on drums.

But that wasn't the only creative thing in the village! The "Uriduck.de" a small advertising bollard car praised the little things that can "catch what goes in at the top and comes out at the bottom". If every man had something like this with him, you could simply spend the night somewhere on the meadow again...

By the way, it is also available for ladies, I just can't tell what the little duck looks like anymore...

So, what else is important to know?

Oh yes, there is actually both a **Volksbank** (Hauptstraße 23) and a **Sparkasse** (Schenefelder Str. 1). Getting supplies of cash shouldn't be a big challenge either.

Even for Die-hard medieval and LARP fans (oh dear, I'm the total beginner regarding these) there's the **BATTLE-MERCHANT**.

Those who are more traditionally minded will be delighted by the **WACKEN CAFE**, with original WACKEN CAFFEE and cake...

Well, already exhausted from reading? Well, then take the bus shuttle and treat yourself to a little (reading) break.

16 - THE SWIMMING POOL

Well, for this area I can unfortunately not yet serve with my own experiences, because I didn't make it to the swimming pool last year, or rather I shied away from the road and preferred to "hang out in the village".

Nevertheless, I would like to warmly recommend it to you, because the weather may be hot this year, too, that cooling down in the swimming pool is a good idea.

If you don't plan to walk all the way anyway, you can also use the W:O:A Pool Shuttle to the swimming pool. After all the hiking on the festival grounds, probably not the most traffic-bound thing you can treat yourself to.

With reference to the photos and reports that I have seen and read on the subject of swimming pools, you will not simply enjoy a "normal" visit to a swimming pool, because there, too, of course, something's going on here! After all, the festival visitors in the swimming pool don't suddenly turn into normal outdoor pool visitors.

Even if you don't have any swimsuits with you: no problem,

because you are in WACKEN. Here you can also deal with "naked facts".

The main thing is to have fun - not at the expense of others, but for everyone!

17 - SHOPPING

By that I don't mean the normal shopping, but the fun of searching for certain fan articles, which you can't find everywhere.

The shops and shopping possibilities in the village are already mentioned in the chapter "The village", so I will not repeat them here again.

I rather invite you to take some time in between to simply stroll around the site. The offers are so varied and numerous that you will always discover something new. In each area there are shops specially tailored to the topics there. Of course, the WASTELAND and WACKINGER VILLAGE areas are particularly exciting.

Since I can't say which individual shops are there this year anyway, just take a little walk and find out by yourself what they have to offer this year. I am sure you will find something suitable!

18 – WHAT'S YOUR FAVORITE BAND?

Last year I had absolutely no answer to this question, which I was asked very seriously at 3:00 in the night at the lockers next to the post office - just big question marks in my head. Oh shit, which band am I actually?

Well, if you bought your card for WACKEN2019 yourself and with full consciousness, then you will probably only smile tiredly if they ask you this question and immediately have some band names ready.

But maybe you just "got into it" and can't come up with a band. Maybe it's because you haven't even had a chance to see which bands will be at the start this year.

Well, then NOW it's just the right moment, because with over 150 bands and concerts plus an extensive supporting program, it definitely makes sense to pick out the most important gigs beforehand.

So that you have the latest information, here's the link to the official WACKEN page:

https://www.wacken.com/en/program/running-order-music/

As with all information, the WACKEN organizers have come up with something here too!

So that you can take advantage of this opportunity, here is a guided tour...

If you click on the link above, you will get to the page with the RUNNING ORDER from 31.07. - 03.08.2019. Yes, it's true, the program starts before the official start of the festival on 01.08.2019. This is also the reason why so many people arrive much earlier, for example on Monday or Tuesday.

Let's start with the HISTORY STAGE as an example. Here the concert series starts on Wednesday, the 31.07.2019 with the band "April Weeps". Since I was born in April, we just follow this band now. Directly below the stage name is the time you can enter the area in front of the stage. In this case this is at 10:30. The band starts their gig at 12:00 and plays for half an hour. After that there is a half hour break and then the concert of the band "Koma" starts at 13:00. In the same rhythm it continues until 23:30. The day ends with the GIG of the band "Baby Heartless".

If you - like me - should ask yourself who these "April weeps" are, you can simply click on the band name and voilà: You see a photo of the band

Author's note: she looks into the camera from the dark fog quite reproachfully...

and to the right of it the Running Order, the Stage, the day of the performance and time.

If you want to know more about the band, you can follow them on the usual social media channels. In this case on
- homepage
- Facebook
- instagram
- Youtube

Quiet easily you land directly on the respective platform with a single click!

My respect for the organizational performance of the festival organizers enlarges with every chapter I write!

Thank you WACKEN-TEAM!!!

Supplementary you can see the top tracks of "April Weeps" beneath the social media channels.

Each with a short excerpt from the song and the forwarding to the platform where you can listen to it in full length.

Below the photo of the band there is a Youtube video with the current song and below a detailed text with further information about the band and their history, the country of origin and the albums.

In order not to write any crap here, I just spontaneously checked one of the other bands listed for this stage and ended up at "Katia". The information here is a bit less extensive: beside a photo of the band

Author's note: really cute, how the three guys look at one behind their beer

the running order with stage, day and time, as well as the social media channels there is "only" the description text of the band here.

Next check: the information about the bands on the HEADBANGERS STAGE. The doors open already on 31.07.2019 at 10:30, but the first concert starts at 13:45 p.m. and lasts twice as long as at the HISTORY STAGE, namely one whole hour. The rebuilding times are much longer, the next band will play at 16:15, the end of the concert series of the first day will be at 1:00 at night.

Okay, so much for the basics! Then have fun picking YOUR bands and getting a first overview (or a second or third if you've already started)

19 - STAGES

WACKEN PLAZA

This is the main link between the campsite and the stage area. But even here there are some really cool stages:

WELCOME TO THE JUNGLE

(cosy Paragu stage)
o Spoken Word Performances + Co.

BULLHEAD CITY CIRCUS

(gigantic big tent)
o W:E:T STAGE
o HEADBANGERS STAGE

Both stages are not bound to special genres, but cover the complete spectrum of the metal world.

WACKINGER VILLAGE & WASTELAND

WACKINGER STAGE - HISTORY STAGE

- o Medieval skirt
- o Pagan Metal
- o folk

WASTELAND STAGE

- o Trash
- o Industrial Metal

WACKEN CENTER:

BEERGARDEN STAGE

o This is where the now famous WACKEN Volunteer Fire Brigade music procession performs, and where several films are shown on the video wall next to the stage.

METAL CHURCH

(in the village church WACKEN)

The Metal Church is only available as a concert hall on Wednesday, 31.07.2019 and only for two concerts.

The first concert will be played by the group Fairytale, whose music is truly magical. They take you on a magical sound adventure, based on the "Elf Throne of Thorsagon" they created "The FantasyMusical". Watching the video on your PC parallel to writing these lines gives me goose bumps!

Definitely the Metal Church is a very suitable location for such a band.

Playtime: 18:00 – 18:45

Wow, that's gonna be great!

The second appearance in the Metal Church will be played by Uli Jon Roth, who left the SCORPIONS in 1978 after 4 studio albums and the live classic TOKYO TAPES. He is now regarded as the forefather of relevant crosses between classic and rock.

When I watch the video of his performance in WACKEN2017 he will probably make METAL CHURCH roar!

His performance takes place: 19:00 – 20:00

I'm already very excited!

INFIELD - HOLY GROUND

The main stages will be opened on Thursday, 01.08.2019:

FASTER

o Opens its doors at 14:00, the first concert Skyline will take place from 14:30 – 15:30. The last concert on Thursday will be played by the band "Sabaton", concert end at midnight.

HARDER

o Also opens its doors at 14:00, but the first concert doesn't start until 15:45, because the stages FASTER and HARDER are played on both sides during the day. If the FASTER is converted, the next concert will take place on HARDER and vice versa. "Sabaton" will then use both stages simultaneously from 22:00 – 0:00!
Definitely a real highlight!

LOUDER

o Things are a bit more contemplative on Thursday on stage LOUDER, the first concert with "Versengold" starts at 14:30. After the "Boss Hoss" from 20:00 – 21:30 the LOUDER stage will be closed.

20 – BANDS

(according to their mentioning on Wacken official website)

A
Aborym
Acranius
Acres
Airbourne
Alabam Black Snakes
All Hail The Yeti
Angelus Apatrida
Anthrax
April Weeps
Archaic
Asrock
Athica
Avatar
Awakening Sun
Axxis

B

Baby Face Nelson
Baby Heartless
Bai Bang
Battle Beast
Beyond the Black
Black Stone Cherry
Blechblos'n
Bleed From Within
Bloodywood
Body Count feat. Ice-T
Brass Against
Brenner
Brothers Of No One
Bullet for My Valentine
Burning Witches

C

Cancer
Cesair
Christopher Bowes and His Plate of Beans
Chumatskyi Shlyah
Coppelius
Cradle of Filth
Crazy Lixx
Crematory
Crisix
Critical Mess
Crobot

D

D-A-D
Damnation Defaced
Dampfmaschine
Dark Funeral
Deathstars
Deine Cousine
Delain
Demons & Wizards
Der Fluch des Drachen
Diamond Head
Diary of Dreams
Die beschissenen Sechs
Die From Sorrow
Die Happy
Die Kassierer
Dirty Shirt
Doch Chkae
Downfall of Gaia
Dragony
Dream Spirit
Drunken Buddha
Drunken Swallows
Duivelspack

E

Eclipse
Eisbrecher
Eluveitie
Emil Bulls
Equilibrium

Evergrey
Extrabreit

F
Facing The Gallows
Fairytale
Fall of Order
Fiddlers's Green
Fight The Fight
For I Am King
Frog Leap

G
Gama Bomb
Gernotshagen
Girlschool
Gloryful
Gloryhammer
Goat Ripper
Grave
Greyface
Grog

H
Hamerferd
Hammerfall
Harpyie
Hellhammer performed by Tom Warrior's Triumph of Death
Helsott

Hämatom

J
Jared James Nichols
Jinjer

K
Kärbholz
Kaizaa
Katla
Koma
Krokus
Kvelertak

L
Lagerstein
Legion Of The Damned
Leviathan
Life of Agony
Lionheart
Lucifer Star Machine

M
Mambo Kurt
Manticora
Meshuggah
Michale Graves

Molllust
Monarch
Mono Inc.
Monstagon
Morpholith
Mr. Hurley & Die Pulveraffen
Myrath

N
Nachtblut
Nailed To Obscurity
Naked Six
Nashville Pussy
Nasty
Necrophobic
Night In Gales
Nordjevel

O
Of Mice & Men
Operus
Opeth

P
Paddy and The Rats
Parkway Drive
Powerwolf
Primal Creation
Primordial

Prong
Prophets of Rage

Q
Queensryche

R
Rage
Ragnaröek
Reckless Love
Reliquiae
Ritual de Nacimiento
Rose Tattoo

S
Sabaton
Santiano
Saor
Savage Messiah
Saxon
Septicflesh
Sibiir
SikTh
Skew Siskin
Skyclad
Skyline
Skynd
Skald
Slave to Sirens

Slayer
Soil
Soul Demise
Stoneman
Subway to Sally
Suidakra
Sweet

T

Tanzwut
Taring
Tausend Löwen Unter Feinden
Terradown
TesseracT
Testament
The Adicts
The BossHoss
The Crown
The Damned
The Lazys
The Linewalkers
The Moon And The Nightspirit
The New Roses
The Night Flight Orchestra
The Offering
The O'Reillys and the Paddyhats
The Quireboys
The Rumjacks
The Sinderellas
The Sisters of Mercy
The Slyde

The Vintage Caravan
The Wild!
Thy Art Is Murder
Torment
Trainwreck
Tribulation
tuXedoo

U
UFO
Uli Jon Roth
Unleashed
Uriah Heep

V
Valley of Chrome
Vampire
Vane
Vanishing
Varang Nord
Velvet Viper
Venom Inc.
Veritatem Solam
Versengold
Victims of Madness
Violons Barbares
Vltimas
Vogelfrey

W
Wacken Firefighters
Warkings
Wiegedood
Windhand
Within Temptation
Witt

Z
Zuriaake

21 - WACKEN WITH A HANDICAP

Here comes a really cool chapter! Proudly presenting and spreading the NEWS, which isn't any...WACKEN is also a great experience for Metalheads with a handicap!

As they say so beautifully: nobody is left behind, we take care of everyone, nobody is excluded.

In "normal life" the stairs are unfortunately too long, the ramp (if there is one) too steep, the elevator just out of operation (or never planned for), the door too narrow and so the next one, which would have been wide enough, can't be reached...

Oh, anyone with a handicap knows more than words can say about it.

Author's note: Even as a (former) mother with a pram, I agree...

All now following information has been taken over from the official WACKEN - Homepage.**Basically without liability on my part!**

If you have any questions, suggestions or criticism, please contact **Drees Ringert, +49 4827 999 669 40** directly or send a mail to this email address:

handicap@wacken.com

First of all: You first buy a normal WACKEN ticket, because there are explicitly NO special tickets for metalheads with disabilities. As everybody you are simply a human being!!

If you are in possession of a severely handicapped pass with the mark "B", you may take one accompanying person to the festival free of charge.

What should you consider with your companion?
Well, first of all, that the WACKEN OPEN AIR takes place on a field. So one of the highest hardness levels applies! Since there have been years (e.g. the legendary 2017) in which the entire area has been transformed into a single muddy landscape, you should take a companion with you who is well equipped in terms of muscles and brains so that he can take you creatively and punctually to the desired location.

If the following happened to you too: "nobody is willing to accompany you to WACKEN..." then that doesn't mean that YOU can't go to WACKEN neither.

Stay positive: you can be helped. More precisely, the network of **"Inklusion Muss Laut Sein"** (inclusion has to be loud) offers you the possibility to find a "BUDDIE" to accompany you for the duration of the festival.

Please contact them directly via:

www.i-m-l-s.com

I could imagine that the tears of emotion would shoot into your eyes when you click on the link, because there are many cool metalheads looking at you who quote no less than Mahatma Gandhi: "Strength does not grow from physical strength - rather from unbending will.

Aids and bag registration

Please register all necessary aids and bags in advance at the same email address as above:

handicap@wacken.com

All other information I quote herewith (without guarantee of completeness) from the official WACKEN homepage:

When registering, please observe the following rules:

- You do NOT have to register wheelchairs, rollators, crutches or canes. Insulin and Adrenalin pens are also excluded from this regulation.

- Aids such as push and pull devices, hand bikes, battery-operated support systems and all other attachments, etc. are not allowed. MUST be registered and marked
.
- NO self-made aids are permitted (example: petrol-driven milling machine as a wheelchair pulling device).
Author's note: yes, the "mean" WACKEN visitor is very creative

- Bags or backpacks that you need due to illness and which have to be taken with you into the INFIELD MUST be registered and marked beforehand.

- You can have the registered aids and bags released and marked at the **ThiesMediCenter** stand (**+49 163 788 938 0)** on Campground

A in the WHEELS OF STEEL AREA. Afterwards you can move freely around the whole festival area.

- Please enter your full name and exactly what your aids or bags are and sent them to **handicap@wacken.com**
- Camping chairs or similar are NOT allowed in the whole INFIELD.

The Wheels of Steel Area:

This area is the CAMPGROUND (not only) for wheelchair users and metalheads with disabilities. Over the years, the name has become a catchword, so every real WACKENER knows what it means. *Author's note: You as WACKEN-GREENHORN now also!!!*

The Campground is located at Bokelrehmer Weg (FASTER-HARDER-LOUDER-LANE)
There is an extra area available for metalheads with disabilities. The access from the Bokelrehmer Weg to the tents and the sanitary stations is fixed with plates. Directly opposite the campground is the main entrance to the stages. It is equipped with an increased number of handicapped accessible sanitary containers as well as handicapped accessible mobile toilets. A medical supply store is directly on site.

Rules and requirements:

- For camping on the campground one of the following markings is necessary in the severely handicapped pass: **G**, **aG**, **B**, **H**, **BL**
- Each Metalhead with a handicap may take a maximum of 4 friends to the Wheels of Steel Area to camp.
- Vehicles over 3,5t are forbidden.
- Like everywhere else, camping is as space-saving as possible, so that everyone can find a place there.

Sanitary facilities:

In addition to the standard sanitary stations, **Campground A** also has barrier-free shower/WC containers. In addition, there are toilets for the disabled all over the festival area and in Shower Camps S2/S3 and in the VIP area. Keys to the facilities will be handed out at the pay kiosk upon presentation of the disabled person pass. They are published in the site plan shortly before the festival.

Additional wheelchair-accessible bathrooms are located in the INFIELD between the main entrance and LOUDER Stage entrance.

Stage platforms:

Hey, good visibility is also a consideration: in front of the stages there are three platforms that allow a better view of the stages in the INFIELD. They are mainly reserved for wheelchair users, otherwise the view of the other fans would be obstructed. In addition, people with an **H** in their severely handicapped pass can be accommodated here. Whether accompanying persons will be allowed on these special stages will be decided on the spot depending on the number of visitors.

Short survey of the signs in the disabled pass:

Since I'm certainly not the only one who doesn't know what to do with the markers (see rules and requirements), I'll add a paragraph here with the corresponding explanations:

G:

The mobility of severely disabled people in road traffic is considerably impaired. Colloquially, the G simply stands for handicapped.
Author's note: the more detailed specification can be found in the Versorgungsmedizin-Verordnung – VersMedV

aG:

Exceptional walking disability
Author's note: More on this can be found in the Ninth Social Code - SGB IX - in §229: Personal Requirements

B:

Accompanying person: this means that the severely disabled person is entitled to take an accompanying person with him/her.
Author's note: More on this in the Ninth Social Code - SGB IX - in §146

H:

Helplessness
Author's note: here you can find more detailed information under §33b of the Income Tax Act (Paragraph 6) or corresponding regulations

BL:

Blind
Author's note: More on this in the Twelfth Social Code - SGB IX - in §72 Paragraph 5

22 – SUPPORTER AREA

This area, in which partner companies present themselves who have been visible for many years or are not yet visible at all, and who are responsible for the success of the WACKENOPENAIR festival, is located close to the BULLHEAD CITY CIRCUSES, between the Place where you receive your entrance sign and the main entrance.

In the new SUPPORTER AREA, meeting spaces will be created with the following service providers, partners and sponsors.

There are many activities to take part in, exciting competitions and helpful offers that are helpful during the daily routine of the festival.

This area will even be open on Monday, 29.07.2019.

SOUNDBOKS

Is a young Danish startup and presents the official W:O:A CAMP LOUDSPEAKER. The W:O:A - Soundboks 2 can be tried out on site or bought right away. In addition, empty batteries can be exchanged for full batteries and you can take part in various activities.

Author's note: nice to look at...and according to a short glimps at the website of Soundboks a real eye-catcher, because it consists of a Wackenlogo!

OHROPAX (inventor of silence)

This company has already established itself in the market and has long become synonymous with hearing protection. Yeahh, again this year every visitor gets two free Ohropax together with the FULL METAL BAG.

GPJOULE (Trust your energy)

Has been a sustainability partner since 2018 and is responsible for finding a solution to meet the energy needs of festival organisers and visitors 100% with renewable energy in the future. You can find out how this will work at their stand.

STAR PETROL STATIONS

This action is making me really curious now, because the announcement is that after the W:O:A - Festival it really starts with the surprises...Since I arrive this time with my own vehicle, this might be a chance to save some money...

The Star LOUNGE awaits us at the festival. There you can charge your smartphone at a lockable mobile phone charging station, take part in a photo campaign, supply yourself with useful festival articles or just chill out in the LOUNGE.

BUNDESWEHR

One of the most energetic helpers on site is the Bundeswehr. Since the festival has the habit of sinking into the mud every now and then and it would often not be possible to drive on the festival grounds without the Bundeswehr.

On site there is also an attractive program and all-day fitness units for all those who don't want to take a break from training during the festival.

Author's note: isn't participation in the festival already sport enough?

WERA TOOLS

The experts at WERA TOOLS not only consistently develop tools further, but always think around the corner.

In the Supporter Area they not only present a selection of their tools but also help with repairs of broken festival equipment in the 1st-Aid-Station and offer many actions to measure forces and participate.

Author's note: have a look at the homepage, there is a scholarship announced every quarter within the framework of a competition!

HOBBY-CARAVAN FACTORY

HOBBY presents a small selection of vehicles at the festival including advice and of course fits perfectly to this festival.

They work closely together with the WACKEN FOUNDATION and have already financed several projects of young metal bands through the auction of HOBBY vehicles.

POHL-BOSKAMP

Hurrah, Pohl-Boskamp again donates GeloRevoise neck tablets for the FULL METAL BAG. Perfect, because the company, which is now THE German manufacturer of neck tablets, has its headquarters just 30 minutes by car from WACKEN.

WAVIN

They celebrate their thirtieth birthday this year, too! The company takes care with its pipes of the transport of drinking water, rainwater and the disposal of waste water. They have also contributed their expertise and products to the famous beer pipeline in the INFIELD and the drains in front of the main stages.

On the occasion of the anniversary, there will be a social media prize draw and an XXL beer pong at the stand.

Author's note: here's also the tip to take a closer look at their website! The SCHACHTDUSCHE listed there is already an eye-catcher!

23 – EVENTS & WARMUPS

Spoken Word

On all days of the festival the WACKEN SLAM BATTLE takes place. The grand finale takes place on Saturday.

Well-known participants:

- Harry Reischmann
- Henry Rollins
- Schnack Ör die
- Torsten Sträter
- Uwe Bahn

Action

Bruchenball Tournament

Cagefights

Fire Show

Kneights Show Combat

Show Combat Training

Warrior's Car Drive and Bike Trail

Party & Walking Acts

Blaas of Glory

A funny formation, that suddenly appears out of nowhere somewhere and shows their show, which you just have to join.

Duivelspack

handmade music comedy with stand up elements

Gaita Mayan

Her music is a combination of the classical medieval - market style and the sound of Central America

Karaoke till Death

Karaoke on BEERGARDEN STAGE, every evening!!! Starting Wednesday

Machine's Late Night Show

Monday and Tuesday at the Landgasthof zur Post in the WACKEN Village, Wednesday at the WELCOME TO THE JUNGLE: W:O:A presenter Machine will review the experiences at the W:O:A every evening with his Late Night Band Alien Rocking Explosion and illustrious guests

Pensen Paletti

Who is on his way with his homemade "Bumm-Guitar"

Metal Disco

for everyone who wants to turn night into day, the Metal Disco will take place with the Hamburg Ballroom DJ collective:

Wednesday:
W:E:T STAGE	time:	1:00 – 3:00
HISTORY STAGE	time:	0:00 – 3:00

Thursday:
HEADBANGERS STAGE	time:	1:00 – 3:00
HISTORY STAGE	time:	0:00 – 3:00

Friday and Saturday:
HISTORY STAGE	time:	0:00 – 3:00

Movies

Extreme Nation

    Moviefield, Thursday: time: 21:00 – 22:30

Heavy Trip

    Moviefield, Wednesday: time: 22:30 – 00:00
    Moviefield, Saturday   time: 22:00 – 23:30

Lords of Chaos

    Moviefield, Thursday: time: 22:30 – 00:30
    Moviefield, Friday: time: 23:45 – 01:45

Short Films

    Moviefield, Wednesday: time: 20:00 – 20:30
    Moviefield, Thursday: time: 20:30 – 21:00
    Moviefield, Friday: time: 20:30 – 21:00
    Moviefield, Saturday: time: 20:00 – 20:30

Syrian Metal is War

    Moviefield, Wednesday: time: 21:00 – 22:30
    Moviefield, Saturday: time: 20:30 – 22:00

The Bitch Movie

    Moviefield, Friday: time: 21:00 – 22:00

The Pursuit of Vikings

    Moviefield, Friday: time: 22:00 – 23:45
    Moviefield, Saturday: time: 23:30 – 01:12

24 - SPORTS

The most brilliant event in my memory of last year has been the METAL YOGA!

Especially because I got into it completely unaware: I strolled comfortably deeply caught in thoughts of where to go next when I suddenly heard a very deep voice and saw muddy, dusty people moving strangely on the ground...and on stage: a wildly smeared fragile woman with a long white-blond braided braid who breathed into the microphone to yoga-like contortions with an infinitely deep voice and then went down...

looking at a devoted crowd of sweaty fans.

I can't say who had more fun: us spectators or the eager yogis on the floor. What was really brilliant was that many units consisted of typical metal movements: Headbanging for example.

If you still have no idea what that should look like, come to WELCOME TO THE JUNGLE – Stage. Take the opportunity to join in as well as just watch from Wednesday to Saturday from 11:00 - 12:00 o'clock.

Have fun!

25 – TIME TO SAY GOODBYE

...it's a little bit like dying...

Well, time to say goodbye! Even this year WACKEN will come to an end at some point. Thousands of dusty characters are exhausted but happily leaving the huge area, still pumped full of adrenaline and infinitely many wonderful memories.

Like a never-ending stream, all the vehicles will be back on the roads towards home, certainly with a lot of melancholy in their hearts, possibly also with a deep longing: for sleep...

It won't be easy to wake up in the "world out there", where people argue, where people run around stressed and where it's so quiet all of a sudden...

Well, I personally would be very happy if you would take a little bit of the WACKEN-FEELING back home with you, continue to live after the VALUES of WACKEN and keep taking care of the well-being of your fellow human beings at home and still go on offering your help to someone who is lying helplessly on the ground.

Well, before we finally feel the pain of saying goodbye, there is one more thing to do!

26 – GET YOUR TICKETS

... for next year!!!
They will be available soon after the end of the festival.

The exact date has not yet been announced. To be safe it's best to sign up for a newsletter to make sure you don't miss it, because experience has shown that tickets sell out very quickly!

After WACKEN is before WACKEN!
Bye Bye - See YOU
on the HOLY GROUND again...

ABOUT THE AUTHOR

Regine Rauin doesn't seem to be a real Hardrock fan at first sight. But this impression is deceptive! She already spent her youth with fans of rock, e.g. at Rock am Ring. In the 80's and 90's she dived into dark, extremely loud pubs in Düsseldorf and enjoyed celebrating together with other enthusiasts to every music that makes the walls quake and the neighbors shiver.

It's especially fun for her to mingle with the leather jackets after a visit to the opera in her evening dress, because she knows that real fans recognize each other that way and that doesn't stop the celebration - fun.

WACKEN 2018 was finally her first live WACKEN experience after long years of "just thinking about going there" and it put all expectations in the shade so much that now, shortly before she is on her way to WACKEN 2019 (the 30th anniversary), she has picked herself up to sit down and write down her experiences and to share her enthusiasm with all the other WACKEN Greenhorns.

NOTES:

Regine Rauin

Made in the USA
Columbia, SC
01 November 2022